# LIVING THE GOSHO

## DAISAKU IKEDA

# LIVING THE GOSHO

DAISAKU IKEDA

World Tribune
—Press—

Published by World Tribune Press
A division of the SGI-USA
606 Wilshire Blvd.
Santa Monica, CA 90401

Cover and interior design by Gopa&Ted2, Inc.

10 9 8 7 6 5 4 3 2 1

ISBN: 978-1-935523-72-7

Library of Congress Control Number:
2014948537

# CONTENTS

# EDITOR'S NOTE

The citations most commonly used in this book have been abbreviated as follows:

LSOC, page number(s) refers to *The Lotus Sutra and Its Opening and Closing Sutras*, translated by Burton Watson (Tokyo: Soka Gakkai, 2009).

OTT, page number(s) refers to *The Record of the Orally Transmitted Teachings,* translated by Burton Watson (Tokyo: Soka Gakkai, 2004).

WND, page number(s) refers to *The Writings of Nichiren Daishonin*, vol. 1 (WND-1) (Tokyo: Soka Gakkai, 1999) and vol. 2 (WND-2) (Tokyo: Soka Gakkai: 2006).

# CHAPTER 1

## The Way of Mentor and Disciple

It must be ties of karma from the distant past that have destined you to become my disciple at a time like this. Shakyamuni and Many Treasures certainly realized this truth. The sutra's statement, "Those persons who had heard the Law dwelled here and there in various Buddha lands, constantly reborn in company with their teachers,"[1] cannot be false in any way.

*"The Heritage of the Ultimate Law of Life"*
(WND-1, 217)

# KOSEN-RUFU:
## THE SHARED JOURNEY
## OF MENTOR AND DISCIPLE

ETERNAL BONDS link mentor and disciple in Buddhism across the three existences of past, present, and future. They are bonds that no one can destroy. As such, we are always reborn together with our teacher in the place where we have a mission to work to fulfill our vow from time without beginning. We earnestly devote our lives to transforming this suffering-filled saha world into a Buddha land pervaded by the four noble virtues of eternity, happiness, true self, and purity. As mentor and disciple, our hearts are always together. Let us strive together and win without fail for the sake of kosen-rufu.

The lion's roar[2] (*shishi ku*) is the preaching of the Buddha. . . . The first *shi* of the word *shishi*, or "lion" [which means "teacher"], is the Wonderful Law that is passed on by the teacher. The second *shi* [which means "child"] is the Wonderful Law as it is received by the disciples. The "roar" is the sound of the teacher and the disciples chanting in unison.

*The Record of the*
*Orally Transmitted Teachings*

(OTT, 111)

# THE LION'S ROAR OF
# THE SHARED COMMITMENT OF
# MENTOR AND DISCIPLE

As DISCIPLES, it's important that we make our mentor's heart our own and let our voices ring out powerfully with our shared commitment to realize the highest good.

The lion's roar of mentor and disciple chanting Nam-myoho-renge-kyo has the unrivaled power to knock back all adversity and transform troubled times.

Because I am the votary of the Lotus Sutra,
I have suffered all manner of persecution at the
hands of the three powerful enemies. How wondrous
that you have, nonetheless, become a disciple
and a supporter of such a person! There must
be some profound reason for our relationship.
Make every possible effort to deepen your faith,
and reach the pure land of Eagle Peak.

*"The Swords of Good and Evil"*

**(WND-1, 451)**

# THE SOLEMN BOND
# OF MENTOR AND DISCIPLE

THE BOND OF mentor and disciple in Buddhism is extremely solemn and profound. Because we have devoted ourselves to the path of the oneness of mentor and disciple—battling and triumphing over hardships together with our mentor—our movement has been able to achieve remarkable development.

I entrust the Soka Gakkai spirit of proud devotion to the path of mentor and disciple to the youth division and future division members, who will be the protagonists of a new age. For this is the path to the eternal victory of kosen-rufu.

You must grit your teeth and never slacken in your faith. Be as fearless as Nichiren when he acted and spoke out before Hei no Saemon-no-jo [the most powerful official in the land].

*"Letter to the Brothers"*

**(WND-1, 498)**

# CONFIDENTLY SPEAKING
# OUT FOR OUR BELIEFS

---

IN ACCORD with this guidance from Nichiren, the first three Soka Gakkai presidents—Tsunesaburo Makiguchi, Josei Toda, and I—have always spoken out for what we believed to be right, no matter whom we were addressing. This is the spirit of the Soka Gakkai.

It is said that Ueno, your deceased father,
was a man of feeling. Since you are his son,
perhaps you have inherited the outstanding qualities
of his character. Blue dye is bluer even than
indigo itself, and ice is colder than water.
How wonderful it is, how wonderful!

*"Offerings in the Snow"*

**(WND-2, 809)**

# CREATING AN ABUNDANT FLOW OF CAPABLE PEOPLE "BLUER THAN INDIGO"

How happy the Daishonin would be to see the growth and valiant efforts of our youth division members! The benefit you are accumulating through your Buddhist practice is immense. As honorable disciples who are "bluer than indigo," please exert yourselves energetically on the path of your mission.

My mentor, President Toda, declared that the Soka Gakkai is the "king of the religious world." And it will be up to you, my young successors, to take the lead of this great organization, and to proudly and courageously expand our movement for kosen-rufu.

I am praying that, no matter how troubled the times
may become, the Lotus Sutra and the ten demon
daughters will protect all of you, praying as earnestly
as though to produce fire from damp wood,
or to obtain water from parched ground.

*"On Rebuking Slander of the Law
and Eradicating Sins"*

**(WND-1, 444)**

# EVERYTHING DEPENDS ON THE VICTORY OF THE DISCIPLE

---

THE DAISHONIN declared that he would resolutely protect his disciples, and he urged them to strive wholeheartedly and win in all endeavors. Taking valiant action to respond to the mentor's call is the path of a disciple in Nichiren Buddhism.

Stones are split open for their hidden gems,
deer are slain for their hides and meat, fish are caught
for their flavor, the kingfisher is killed for its gorgeous
feathers, and a beautiful woman is envied for her
beauty. This is the case with me. Because I am
the votary of the Lotus Sutra, I have suffered
all manner of persecution at the hands
of the three powerful enemies.

*"The Swords of Good and Evil"*

**(WND-1, 451)**

# THE GREAT
## ARE ALWAYS ENVIED

I N ANY AGE, those who stand up for truth and justice are resented and persecuted. It is because they are great that they are envied.

The first three Soka Gakkai presidents, proudly striving with the very same spirit as Nichiren Daishonin, have triumphed over intense hatred and jealousy as predicted in the Lotus Sutra. We have opened a path of trust and friendship that extends around the globe.

Let's ever advance onward, calmly rising above slander and abuse of the kind the Daishonin describes will befall his followers, and establish clear and enduring actual proof of the victory of Soka.

Following me, you, as a votary of the Lotus Sutra,
have told others of this Law. What else could
this be but the transmission of the Law?
Carry through with your faith in the Lotus Sutra.
You cannot strike fire from flint
if you stop halfway.

*"Earthly Desires Are Enlightenment"*
**(WND-1, 319)**

# KEEP MOVING FORWARD
# DAY AFTER DAY

---

E VEN IF IT is just one small step, keep moving forward day after day. Don't get disheartened and don't give up! Let's complete the tasks before us, one thing at a time. It is also important to share our ideals confidently with others. This way of action, we should remember, is the path to the brilliant victory of mentor and disciple.

The Buddha wrote that one should become
the master of one's mind rather than let one's mind
master oneself.[3] This is what I mean when
I emphatically urge you to give up even your body,
and never begrudge even your life for
the sake of the Lotus Sutra.

"Letter to Gijo-bo"

(WND-1, 390)

# STRIVING WITH THE SAME SPIRIT AS OUR MENTOR

---

OUR MINDS CAN be all too easily influenced and swayed by our environment; in striving to master our mind, therefore, it becomes important to seek out and follow the example of a teacher or mentor who can guide us in the correct direction.

When we of Soka strive for kosen-rufu with the same spirit as our mentor in the realm of Buddhism, we can establish an unshakable mountain of faith in our hearts. This is our pride as champions of humanity who are dedicated to the path of mentor and disciple.

I have upheld my faith without faltering, even though . . . the lord of Kamakura [the regent] twice exiled me, and I nearly had my head cut off. Because I have persevered without fear, there are now people who think my teachings may be true.

*"The Royal Palace"*

**(WND-1, 489)**

# THE COURAGEOUS SPIRIT OF NOT BEGRUDGING ONE'S LIFE

---

BECAUSE THE FIRST three Soka Gakkai presidents have truly inherited Nichiren's spirit, we have each faced life-threatening persecutions. Nonetheless, we have not been daunted in the least and have steadfastly walked the path of truth and justice.

Now, people of wisdom and discernment throughout the world have extended their friendship and support to us.

Youth, please carry on this courageous spirit of not begrudging one's life.

# CHAPTER 2

Banner of Victory

Those who believe in the Lotus Sutra are as if
in winter, but winter always turns to spring.
Never, from ancient times on, has anyone heard
or seen of winter turning back to autumn.
Nor have we ever heard of a believer in
the Lotus Sutra who turned into an ordinary
[unenlightened] person.

*"Winter Always Turns to Spring"*

**(WND-1, 536)**

# WINTER ALWAYS TURNS
# TO SPRING

No MATTER HOW cold and bitter the winter, spring will definitely come. All who have faith in the Lotus Sutra will attain Buddhahood without exception. Nichiren Buddhism exists so that those who have suffered the most can achieve happiness. As SGI members, we earnestly take action to help people overcome all kinds of hardships and sufferings and usher in a springtime of hope and victory in their lives.

A sword is useless in the hands of a coward.
The mighty sword of the Lotus Sutra must be
wielded by one courageous in faith.
Then one will be as strong as a demon
armed with an iron staff.

*"Reply to Kyo'o"*
**(WND-1, 412)**

# OPENING THE PATH TO VICTORY WITH THE "SWORD" OF COURAGEOUS FAITH

---

THE INVINCIBLE POWER of the Mystic Law manifests itself through courageous faith. Please open the path to victory with powerful prayer and the indomitable spirit to never be defeated.

In the Latter Day of the Law, the votary of the Lotus Sutra will appear without fail. The greater the hardships befalling him, the greater the delight he feels, because of his strong faith. Doesn't a fire burn more briskly when logs are added?

*"A Ship to Cross the Sea of Suffering"*

(WND-1, 33)

# STRUGGLES BRING FORTH OUR GREATEST STRENGTH

IT IS PRECISELY when we are battling hardships in life that we can bring forth the supreme power of the Buddha from within. All struggles test and prove our strength, leading us to the attainment of Buddhahood.

Nichiren Daishonin urges us to joyfully and courageously tackle problems and difficulties head-on. Simply lamenting our situation will not change it.

Overcoming hardships is essential to attaining enlightenment. That is the foundation of our practice as votaries of the Lotus Sutra. With strong faith, let's enact joyful dramas of transforming karma and write a magnificent history of human revolution.

Each of you should summon up the courage
of a lion king and never succumb to threats from
anyone. The lion king fears no other beast,
nor do its cubs. Slanderers are like barking
foxes, but Nichiren's followers
are like roaring lions.

*"On Persecutions Befalling the Sage"*
**(WND-1, 997)**

# LEADING AN INVINCIBLE LIFE

PRACTICING NICHIREN BUDDHISM empowers us without end. The "courage of a lion king" resides within our own lives. Anyone who chants Nam-myoho-renge-kyo can summon forth that courage without fail.

When we brim with the "courage of a lion king," the howling clamor of slander and abuse will not intimidate us. Let's live out our lives with confidence and pride, unbeaten by any trials.

Could not this illness of your husband's be
the Buddha's design, because the Vimalakirti
and Nirvana sutras both teach that sick people
will surely attain Buddhahood? Illness gives rise
to the resolve to attain the way .

"The Good Medicine for All Ills"
(WND-1, 937)

# NEVER BE DEFEATED BY ILLNESS

ILLNESS DOES NOT equal unhappiness. Illness itself can provide us with an opportunity to develop a more profound state of life and to fundamentally transform our karma. This is the way of faith for attaining Buddhahood in this lifetime. Therefore, though we may experience ill health, it's important that we stay strong and resolute in spirit.

The Daishonin affirms that "sick people will surely attain Buddhahood." We can definitely transform poison into medicine. With the lion's roar of Nam-myoho-renge-kyo, we can triumph over all illness.

I am wholeheartedly chanting for the well-being and long lives of all our members.

At times we are born as human beings, becoming
rulers of various countries, high ministers, court
nobles, or other court officials, and we think ourselves
incomparably happy. Thus we content ourselves with
such little gains and are delighted with them.
However, the Buddha has taught that these
accomplishments are mere prosperity in a dream,
a phantom joy, and that we should simply
accept and uphold the Lotus Sutra
and quickly become Buddhas.

*"Sovereign, Teacher, and Parent"*

**(WND-2, 36)**

# THE PRIDE OF CHAMPIONS
# OF HUMANITY

---

POWER, MATERIAL wealth, and fame are fleeting; they can easily disappear. We must not be swayed by such superficial trappings. As individuals working to spread the eternal Mystic Law, we are drawing forth the indestructible life state of eternity, happiness, true self, and purity from within while helping others do the same. We are leading lives of absolute victory. Our hearts are filled with the pride of champions of humanity.

It is extremely rare to be born as a human being.
Not only are you endowed with human form, but you
have had the rare fortune to encounter Buddhism.
Moreover, out of the Buddha's many teachings you
have encountered the daimoku, or the title,
of the Lotus Sutra and become its votary.
Truly you are a person who has offered alms
to a hundred thousand million Buddhas
in his past existences!

*"Letter to Jakunichi-bo"*

(WND-1, 993)

# PUTTING DETERMINATIONS
# INTO ACTION

As a result of profound karmic ties from the past, we have had the good fortune to be born as human beings and to encounter the teaching of the Mystic Law, which is difficult to encounter. How precious is our existence! We must not spend this life in vain and be left with regrets.

Each one of our struggles and hardships for kosen-rufu will become a joy-filled "memory of your present life in this human world" (WND-1, 64)—indestructible, diamond-like treasures of the heart. In the realm of Buddhism, none of our efforts is ever wasted. Let's adorn our lives with victory after victory, always putting our determinations into action without delay.

Can anything exceed the sun and moon in brightness?
Can anything surpass the lotus flower in purity?
The Lotus Sutra is the sun and moon and the lotus
flower. Therefore it is called the Lotus Sutra of the
Wonderful Law. Nichiren, too, is like the sun
and moon and the lotus flower.

*"Easy Delivery of a Fortune Child"*
**(WND-1, 186)**

# SHINE WITH THE BRILLIANCE
# OF THE SUN AND
# THE LOTUS FLOWER

---

THE NAME of the young women's division group "Kayo-kai" (lit. Flower Sun Group) carries profound meaning as it signifies both the brightness of the sun and moon and the purity of the lotus flower. It embodies the power of the Mystic Law that can overcome any adversity.

I hope that each young woman will shine her brightest as members of the Kayo-kai and become champions of happiness.

If votaries of the Lotus Sutra . . . practice as the sutra
directs, then every one of them without exception
will surely attain Buddhahood within his or her
present lifetime. To cite an analogy, if one plants
the fields in spring and summer, then, whether
it be early or late, one is certain to reap
a harvest within the year.
Votaries of the Lotus Sutra fall into three categories,
superior, middling, and inferior, depending upon their
capacities, and yet all will invariably attain
enlightenment within a single lifetime.

*"The Doctrine of Three Thousand Realms in
a Single Moment of Life"*

**(WND-2, 88)**

# BUDDHISM MEANS
# WINNING IN THE END

---

Nichiren Daishonin states that all people are assured of attaining Buddhahood, and that this is "without exception." Though we may not see results immediately, by persevering in our Buddhist practice we can definitely win and open the way forward in our lives.

Everything is part of our practice. Everything in our life has profound meaning in terms of Buddhism; it is there to make us even stronger and develop a life of greater depth.

The heart of Nichiren Buddhism is to chant to the Gohonzon for lasting victory and joyfully adorn the closing chapter of our life with triumph.

[In China long ago,] T'ai-kung Wang undertook to invade the Yin realm because the Earl of the West had treated him with due courtesy, and Chang Liang weighed how to overthrow the Ch'in dynasty because he was moved by the sincerity of the king of Han. These men were both fitted to the age and gained proper recognition. Thus within the tents of command they were able to devise strategies that assured victory a thousand miles away.

*"The Day before Yesterday"*

**(WND-2, 391)**

# THOROUGH PREPARATION IS
# THE KEY TO VICTORY

---

WISE LEADERS are able to bring forth the inherent potential of others.

Sincerity is the foremost requirement for leaders of the SGI. Victory will be determined by prayer based on a powerful vow for kosen-rufu, thorough discussion, and initiative taken by our leaders.

I hope that all leaders will act on my behalf, taking exemplary leadership to advance our movement for kosen-rufu.

Devadatta was the foremost good friend to the Thus Come One Shakyamuni. In this age as well, it is not one's allies but one's powerful enemies who assist one's progress.

*"The Actions of the Votary of the Lotus Sutra"*
**(WND-1, 770)**

# TAKE ON POWERFUL ENEMIES WITH COURAGE AND JOY

Youth, take on powerful enemies with courage and joy!

A heart that shies away from painful challenges and avoids hardships only strengthens devilish functions and allows them to take advantage.

By boldly challenging powerful enemies, we can forge and polish our lives. It enables us to do our human revolution and achieve Buddhahood in this lifetime.

As SGI members, directly connected to Nichiren Daishonin, let us "summon up the courage of a lion king" (WND-1, 997) and fearlessly and confidently triumph over all.

# CHAPTER 3

# Single-Minded Determination

Nam-myoho-renge-kyo is like the roar of a lion.
What sickness can therefore be an obstacle?
It is written that those who embrace the daimoku
of the Lotus Sutra will be protected by the
Mother of Demon Children and by
the ten demon daughters.

*"Reply to Kyo'o"*

**(WND-1, 412)**

# TRIUMPHING OVER ILLNESS WITH THE LION'S ROAR OF NAM-MYOHO-RENGE-KYO

No ONE CAN avoid battling illness at some point in life. But the lion's roar of Nam-myoho-renge-kyo is invincible. The supreme power of our chanting enables us to bring forth the boundless life force of the lion king from within us. No illness can ever destroy the happiness of a dedicated champion of kosen-rufu.

I hope, therefore, that you will chant with courage and fierce determination, positively transform your situation in accord with the principle of changing poison into medicine and resolutely triumph over all. I am always chanting fervently that the protective functions of the universe will thoroughly protect my beloved fellow members everywhere.

When once we chant Myoho-renge-kyo,[4] with just
that single sound we summon forth and manifest
the Buddha nature of all Buddhas; all existences;
all bodhisattvas; all voice-hearers; all the deities
such as Brahma, Shakra, and King Yama;
the sun and moon, and the myriad stars;
the heavenly gods and earthly deities,
on down to hell-dwellers, hungry spirits,
animals, asuras, human and
heavenly beings, and all other living beings.
This blessing is immeasurable
and boundless.

*"How Those Initially Aspiring to the Way Can
Attain Buddhahood through the Lotus Sutra"*
**(WND-1, 887)**

# STRIVING TO AWAKEN AND SUMMON FORTH THE BUDDHA NATURE OF ALL PEOPLE

L ET'S KEEP CHANTING Nam-myoho-renge-kyo steadfastly and take action to move forward. Our efforts for kosen-rufu constitute a great struggle for good aimed at awakening and summoning forth the Buddha nature of all people.

Since you now appear certain to attain Buddhahood,
perhaps the heavenly devil and evil spirits are using
illness to try to intimidate you. Life in this
world is limited. Never be even the least bit afraid!
And you demons, by making this man suffer,
are you trying to swallow a sword point first,
or embrace a raging fire, or become the
archenemy of the Buddhas of the
ten directions in the three existences?

"The Proof of the Lotus Sutra"
**(WND-1, 1109)**

# FAITH FOR
# OVERCOMING ILLNESS

---

NICHIREN DAISHONIN fiercely admonishes the devil of illness attacking his young disciple.

To those of you who are ill, please be reassured that the Daishonin is surely on your side and that your mentor and many fellow members are chanting for you. Don't let ill health defeat you. Everything you are going through now is a trial that will enable you to ultimately attain Buddhahood. Please chant with strong resolve. Confronted with the lion's roar of Nam-myoho-renge-kyo, even the devil of illness will turn tail and flee.

Please draw forth the boundless life state of Buddhahood, with the deep determination to live out your life to the fullest for the sake of kosen-rufu.

There are not two lands, pure or impure in
themselves. The difference lies solely
in the good or evil of our minds.

*"On Attaining Buddhahood in This Lifetime"*
**(WND-1, 4)**

## ALL PEOPLE POSSESS THE POWER
## FOR TRANSFORMATION

WHEN WE OURSELVES change, our environment changes too. Through our individual human revolution, we can transform our community and society into a "pure land." Such efforts are the very essence of our great people's movement of kosen-rufu.

So long as one maintains firm faith, one is
certain to receive the great protection of
the gods. I say this for your sake. I know
your faith has always been admirable,
but now you must strengthen it
more than ever.

*"The Supremacy of the Law"*

**(WND-1, 614)**

# STRENGTHEN YOUR FAITH
# MORE THAN EVER

---

THE HUMAN HEART is a wondrous thing. We can strengthen and deepen our heart without limit. And faith is its strongest and deepest expression.

No matter what our circumstances may be, when we have firm faith in the Mystic Law, we will definitely be protected by the positive functions of the universe.

In Nichiren Buddhism, faith means always looking to the future and making a fresh start from this moment on. Let's begin each day anew with the resolve to strengthen our faith more than ever. This is the essence of the proud ever-victorious spirit of the SGI.

Never seek this Gohonzon outside yourself.
The Gohonzon exists only within the mortal flesh
of us ordinary people who
embrace the Lotus Sutra and chant
Nam-myoho-renge-kyo.

*"The Real Aspect of the Gohonzon"*

**(WND-1, 832)**

# THE GOHONZON EXISTS WITHIN US

THE GOHONZON EXISTS within us. The supremely noble life state of Buddhahood shines nowhere but in our own lives as people dedicated to the cause of kosen-rufu. Consequently, no matter what happens, as long as we maintain strong faith, we will be fine. There is nothing to worry about. Nothing is more precious than the individual human beings who uphold and practice the Mystic Law.

Misfortune will change into fortune.
Muster your faith, and pray to this Gohonzon.
Then what is there that cannot be achieved?

*"Reply to Kyo'o"*
**(WND-1, 412)**

# CHANGING POISON INTO MEDICINE THROUGH POWERFUL PRAYER

THE BUDDHISM of Nichiren Daishonin allows us to change poison into medicine and to transform our negative karma. There is no hardship or suffering that we cannot overcome, no darkness that we cannot break through. Now is the time to bring forth the vast and immeasurable power of the Buddha and the Law.

The more challenging the times, the more important it is that we take a step forward based on powerful prayer. Courageous faith is the very heart of Nichiren Buddhism.

When one becomes aware of the Buddha
vehicle within oneself, one can enter the palace
of oneself [Buddhahood]. Chanting
Nam-myoho-renge-kyo is what is meant
by entering the palace of oneself.

*The Record of the*
*Orally Transmitted Teachings*
**(See OTT, 209)**

# THE PALACE OF OUR LIFE
## IS INDESTRUCTIBLE

WE WHO CHANT Nam-myoho-renge-kyo are ourselves Buddhas. A magnificent palace exists in the depths of our being—a palace that no one can destroy and nothing can desecrate.

Bringing our lives to shine and working to create beautiful realms of peace and happiness in our beloved communities—this is the invincible spirit of establishing the correct teaching for the peace of the land.

*Myo* means to revive, that is, to return to life.

*"The Daimoku of the Lotus Sutra"*

**(WND-1, 149)**

# FAITH IN NICHIREN BUDDHISM IS A SOURCE OF LIMITLESS HOPE

WHEN WE LIVE our lives based on faith in Nichiren Buddhism, then no matter what our situation or where we may find ourselves, it is possible for us to make a fresh beginning from there, to open the way to a future of limitless hope from that moment.

Buddhism enables us to revive our spirits and revitalize our communities, allowing us to create happy lives without fail and help others do the same. That is the purpose of Buddhism.

From this single element of mind spring all the various
lands and environmental conditions. The sacred
teachings of the Buddha's lifetime are devoted
to explaining this principle. These are what is known
as the storehouse of the eighty-four thousand
teachings. All these are teachings encompassed
within the single entity of an individual.
Hence the storehouse of the eighty-four thousand
teachings represents a day-to-day record
of one's own existence.

*"The Unanimous Declaration by the Buddhas
of the Three Existences"*

**(WND-2, 843)**

# WRITING A GOLDEN RECORD OF OUR LIFE DAY AFTER DAY

EVERYTHING STARTS from our inner determination. However dark the times, when the sun of time without beginning—our inner Buddhahood—rises in our heart, we can transform even our environment. No matter what happens, the important thing is not to despair, not to give up, and never to let oneself be defeated.

As proud members of the SGI, we are joyfully writing a golden record of our life day after day.

Chudapanthaka was unable to memorize a teaching of
fourteen characters even in the space of three years,
and yet he attained Buddhahood. Devadatta, on the
other hand, had committed to memory sixty thousand
teachings but fell into the hell of incessant suffering.
These examples exactly represent the situation in
the world in this present latter age. Never suppose
that they pertain only to other people and
not to yourselves.

*"Three Tripitaka Masters Pray for Rain"*
**(WND-1, 602)**

# FAITH IS THE KEY

---

IN THE REALM of Buddhism, those who are honest and sincere will undoubtedly win in the end. There is no way that those who strive for kosenrufu with dedication, perseverance, and earnestness throughout their lives will fail to become happy. The victorious lives of our honorable fellow members are the most powerful testimony to this truth. In contrast, arrogant people with positions of great responsibility who forget their debts of gratitude, seeking only personal fame and fortune, travel a path that leads to misery in accord with the strict law of cause and effect.

The key to attaining Buddhahood in this lifetime is faith alone.

We ordinary people can see neither our own
eyelashes, which are so close, nor the heavens
in the distance. Likewise, we do not see
that the Buddha exists in
our own hearts.

*"New Year's Gosho"*
**(WND-1, 1137)**

# THE SUPREME LIFE STATE OF
# THE BUDDHA EXISTS WITHIN US

---

WHAT DOES IT MEAN to know one's true self?—Nichiren Buddhism offers a clear answer to this enduring question of human existence.

Even when confronted with painful karma and finding ourselves feeling discouraged, as practitioners of Nichiren Buddhism we can get back on our feet with confidence and dignity again and again. This is because we know that the supreme life state of the Buddha exists within us.

Everything is decided by our mind and attitude in each moment. Let's wholeheartedly chant Nammyoho-renge-kyo with the conviction that "I am a Buddha," and cheerfully and energetically live out our lives true to ourselves.

What is most important is that, by chanting
Nam-myoho-renge-kyo alone, you can attain
Buddhahood. It will no doubt depend
on the strength of your faith. To have faith
is the basis of Buddhism.

*"The Real Aspect of the Gohonzon"*

**(WND-1, 832)**

# FAITH IS THE BASIS
# FOR EVERYTHING

FAITH IN THE Mystic Law is the basis for victory. Those who continue to chant Nam-myoho-renge-kyo through all are admirable and strong without compare. When we resolutely bring forth the power of faith and practice, we can manifest the boundless power of the Buddha and the Law in our lives.

No matter what the situation, first chant. Chanting Nam-myoho-renge-kyo is the ultimate driving force that enables us to break through all obstacles, undefeated by any problem or suffering.

The lion king is said to advance three steps, then gather himself to spring, unleashing the same power whether he traps a tiny ant or attacks a fierce animal. In inscribing this Gohonzon for her protection, Nichiren was like the lion king. This is what the sutra means by "the power [of the Buddhas] that has the lion's ferocity."[5]

*"Reply to Kyo'o"*

(WND-1, 412)

# A GATHERING OF LIONHEARTED CHAMPIONS IN FAITH

To give one's wholehearted attention to even the smallest task or matter, to not grow careless or negligent, to approach challenges with the determination to succeed, and to win out through all—this is the essential spirit of the lion king.

The SGI is a gathering of such lionhearted champions in faith. The sound of our chanting of Nam-myoho-renge-kyo is a powerful lion's roar that can vanquish all obstacles and devilish functions. Enabling us to summon forth wisdom and courage from within, our practice of chanting is the fundamental means for achieving absolute victory.

# CHAPTER 4

## Garden of Dialogue

If one gives food to others, one will improve
one's own lot, just as, for example, if one lights a fire
for others, one will brighten one's own way.

"On the Three Virtues of Food"

(WND-2, 1060)

# BE A BRIGHT SOURCE OF ENCOURAGEMENT

Youth, be strong, wise, and cheerful! With passion and enthusiasm, create positive value for peace, justice, and the happiness of all.

Be individuals who shine as a bright source of encouragement, earnestly praying for the happiness of your friends and sincerely engaging them in dialogue.

As youth, the light that you generate through each of your heartfelt deeds and actions gives others courage and hope for the possibility of a brilliant future.

Treating one's friends with courtesy means that,
although one may encounter them ten or twenty times
in the course of a single day, one greets
them courteously as though they had traveled
a thousand or two thousand miles to see one,
never showing them indifference.

*"The Four Virtues and
the Four Debts of Gratitude"*
**(WND-2, 636)**

# COURTESY IS THE HALLMARK OF CULTURE

L ET'S EXPAND our bonds of friendship. When
we welcome or visit friends, let's make it a
heartfelt encounter based on genuine courtesy and
respect. This is the spirit we should have as practitioners of Nichiren Buddhism.

Courtesy is the hallmark of culture. Arrogance is
the way of oppression, whereas sincerity is the way
of honor. Let us always advance and win based on
humanism.

It is due to the authority and supernatural power
of Bodhisattva Universal Worthy that this Lotus Sutra
is propagated throughout Jambudvipa [the entire
world]. Therefore the widespread propagation
of this sutra must be under the care and protection
of Bodhisattva Universal Worthy.

*The Record of the*
*Orally Transmitted Teachings*
**(OTT, 190)**

# WORLD PEACE AND THE POWER OF BODHISATTVA UNIVERSAL WORTHY

WE ARE COMMITTED to creating peace through dialogue, infused with a universal wisdom, as exemplified by Bodhisattva Universal Worthy. We have now entered an age when many of the world's leading scholars find resonance with the value-creating philosophy of the SGI.

Real wisdom is free from boastful arrogance or an attitude of superiority. The wise and noble spirit of Bodhisattva Universal Worthy pulses in the commitment to work for the welfare and happiness of people and in efforts for the sake of truth and justice.

Student division members, now is the time to devote yourselves wholeheartedly to learning. Talk confidently with others about Nichiren Buddhism. Brightly illuminate the future of humanity with the great light of wisdom in action.

When one who is able to show clearly visible proof
in the present expounds the Lotus Sutra, there
also will be persons who will believe.

*"Letter to Horen"*

**(WND-1, 512)**

# NOTHING SPEAKS LOUDER
# THAN ACTUAL PROOF

---

NOTHING IS MORE eloquent than actual proof. That's why it is important that we strive to steadily demonstrate actual proof of our victory in society.

Relating such experiences to others is one of the most powerful ways to advance kosen-rufu.

Now for the past twenty-eight years, since the fifth year of the Kencho era [1253], cyclical sign *mizunoto-ushi,* the twenty-eighth day of the fourth month,[6] until the present, the twelfth month of the third year of the Koan era [1280], cyclical sign *kanoe-tatsu,* I, Nichiren, have done nothing else, but have labored solely to put the five or seven characters of Myoho-renge-kyo[7] into the mouths of all the living beings of the country of Japan.

*"On Reprimanding Hachiman"*

**(WND-2, 931)**

# THE WISH FOR THE
# HAPPINESS OF ALL HUMANITY

NICHIREN DAISHONIN persevered in his
selfless struggle to spread the Mystic Law,
driven solely by his wish for people's happiness. We,
who have inherited this noble mission, are all esti-
mable Bodhisattvas of the Earth and emissaries of
the Buddha of the Latter Day of the Law endowed
with "great good fortune from past existences"
(LSOC, 356).

Today, countless valiant young Bodhisattvas of
the Earth are emerging one after another. As we
continue to spread the Mystic Law by reaching out
in dialogue to as many people as possible, let's scale
fresh summits of kosen-rufu.

Teaching another something is the same as oiling
the wheels of a cart so that they turn even though
it is heavy, or as floating a boat on water
so that it moves ahead easily.

*"The Wealthy Man Sudatta"*

**(WND-1, 1086)**

## SHARING OTHERS' SUFFERINGS AND CONCERNS IS THE SPIRIT OF THE SOKA GAKKAI

LIFE'S SUFFERINGS and concerns are many and diverse. Therefore, it is crucial to impart warm words of encouragement that reach each person's heart. Taking on people's problems as our own, chanting together, and pushing ahead with them by working side by side for kosen-rufu—this spirit of empathy and care is the fundamental spirit of the Soka Gakkai.

Please genuinely listen to others. When you sincerely chant for someone else's happiness, you can draw out heartfelt words of wisdom. It is also important to bring forth the courage to keep moving forward yourself and inspire those you are supporting to do the same.

When the bodhisattva Never Disparaging makes his
bow of obeisance to the four kinds of believers,
the Buddha nature inherent in the four kinds of
believers of overbearing arrogance bows in obeisance
to the bodhisattva Never Disparaging. It is like
the situation when one faces a mirror and makes
a bow of obeisance: the image in the mirror
likewise makes a bow of obeisance
to oneself.

*The Record of the
Orally Transmitted Teachings*

**(OTT, 165)**

# WHEN WE CHANGE,
# OUR ENVIRONMENT CHANGES

---

No one is stronger than a person who has steadfastly chanted Nam-myoho-renge-kyo, the very essence of Nichiren Daishonin's teachings. There is nothing more honorable or empowering than chanting for the happiness of others. Our capacity to chant for the happiness of others itself is a reflection of the life state of Buddhahood.

When we change, those in our environment will definitely change too. Conversations in which we share the greatness of Nichiren Buddhism are infinitely profound interactions that summon forth the Buddha nature in our own lives and the lives of others.

When a tree has been transplanted, though fierce winds may blow, it will not topple if it has a firm stake to hold it up. But even a tree that has grown up in place may fall over if its roots are weak.

*"Three Tripitaka Masters Pray for Rain"*
**(WND-1, 598)**

# ENCOURAGEMENT IMPARTS BOUNDLESS STRENGTH

---

PEOPLE WHO HAVE the support of others are strong. They are undefeatable. With the solid support of good friends, we can weather all storms of adversity to achieve a life of happiness and victory.

Offering encouragement means imparting boundless strength.[8] Having sincere dialogues with others is simple and low key, but it is the way to forge the strongest heart-to-heart bonds and build the most unshakable trust.

The seeds of Buddhahood exist nowhere apart from the Lotus Sutra. If it were possible to attain Buddhahood through the provisional teachings, then why would the Buddha have said that one should insist on preaching the Lotus Sutra, and that both those who slander it and those who believe in it will benefit? Or why would he say, "We care nothing for our bodies or lives [but are anxious only for the unsurpassed way]"[9]? Persons who have set their minds upon the way should clearly understand these matters.

*"How Those Initially Aspiring to the Way Can Attain Buddhahood through the Lotus Sutra"*

**(WND-1, 882)**

# ENGAGING IN DIALOGUE
# FOR THE HAPPINESS OF
# OUR FRIENDS

BY TALKING TO others about the ideals and principles of Nichiren Buddhism, we are sowing the seeds for people's happiness. Let us, therefore, not hesitate to reach out to others in dialogue and share our philosophy with a bright confidence. The sincerity with which we chant for others' happiness will eventually touch their hearts without fail.

Let's joyfully engage in meaningful dialogue, having the courage to communicate our heartfelt convictions.

"[At all times I think to myself]: How can I cause living
beings to gain entry into the unsurpassed way?"[10]
These words express the Buddha's deepest wish
to enable both those who accept the Lotus Sutra and
those who oppose it to attain Buddhahood.
Because this is his ultimate purpose, those
who embrace the Lotus Sutra for even a short while
are acting in accordance with his will. And if they
act in accordance with the Buddha's will,
they will be repaying the debt of gratitude
they owe to the Buddha

"Questions and Answers about Embracing
the Lotus Sutra"

(WND-1, 63)

# COURAGEOUSLY CONNECTING OTHERS TO BUDDHISM

---

THE BUDDHA'S WISH is to help all people attain Buddhahood. By forming a connection with Buddhism, all people will eventually gain true happiness, not only those who embrace faith in the Lotus Sutra but also those who oppose it. This is the source of the Buddha's greatest joy.

Therefore, when we courageously talk to others about our practice for the sake of their happiness, enabling more and more people to form a connection with Buddhism, we are acting with great compassion in accord with the Buddha's true intent.

This principle of the Ten Worlds applies not only to living beings. All things that make up the objective and the subjective worlds, as well as insentient beings such as plants and trees and so on down to the tiniest speck of dust, are every one of them endowed with the Ten Worlds.

*"The Differences between Hinayana and Mahayana"*
**(WND-2, 471)**

# CREATING A CENTURY OF LIFE

Viewed from the true essence of Buddhism, we find that not only human beings but all things in the universe possess the supremely noble Buddha nature. The wisdom to establish the dignity of life as a universal principle and to promote our harmonious coexistence with others, the natural world, and the universe is found in the teaching of the Mystic Law.

Many people around the world are beginning to deeply seek this supreme philosophy. Our grassroots dialogue movement to share the greatness of Nichiren Buddhism is a noble endeavor to make the twenty-first century shine as a century of life.

# CHAPTER 5

# Field of Mission

When one comes to realize and see that each thing—
the cherry, the plum, the peach, the damson—
in its own entity, without undergoing any change,
possesses the eternally endowed three bodies,
then this is what is meant by the word *ryo*,
"to include" or all-inclusive.
Now Nichiren and his followers, who chant
Nam-myoho-renge-kyo, are the original possessors
of these eternally endowed three bodies.

*The Record of the*
*Orally Transmitted Teachings*
**(OTT, 200–201)**

# JOYFULLY PLAY OUT YOUR UNIQUE MISSION

---

YOU UNDOUBTEDLY have a mission that only you can fulfill.

Faith in Nichiren Buddhism enables us to bring out and use in the most positive way the unique attributes that we each possess.

There's no need for you to pretend to be someone else; just be yourself. President Toda taught the importance of living true to oneself. Don't be afraid of expressing your inner potential and never deprecate yourself.

You are all the protagonists in the drama of kosen-rufu. Please brilliantly play out your unique mission in the way that is true to yourself—just like the cherry, plum, peach, and damson.

[Your deceased husband] is probably watching
his wife and children in the heavenly mirrors
of the sun and moon every moment
of the day and night.

*"Winter Always Turns to Spring"*

**(See WND-1, 536)**

# OUR FAMILY BONDS
# ARE EVERLASTING

---

T HE BONDS OF family in the realm of the
Mystic Law are everlasting. We will always be
together with our family members, lifetime after
lifetime.

To those of you who have lost a family member, please think of yourselves as their "successors," appreciating the good fortune they have shared with you and resolving to live out your life to the fullest in their stead. I hope you will fulfill your own great mission in this existence, while forever cherishing them in your heart.

The sutra says, "[They are] unsoiled by worldly things like the lotus flower in the water. Emerging from the earth . . ." Here we see that the Bodhisattvas of the Earth are the lotus of the entity of the Mystic Law, and that the lotus is being used here as a simile.

*"The Entity of the Mystic Law"*

**(WND-1, 431)**

# LIKE THE LOTUS FLOWER

---

L IFE IS A battle with our problems and karma. In the same way that the lotus growing in a muddy swamp brings forth pure and fragrant blossoms, however, we can bring happiness and victory to bloom in our lives and help others do the same. This is the way of the Bodhisattvas of the Earth whose lives are "like the lotus flower in the water" (LSOC, 263).

Those who sincerely chant and actually spread the Mystic Law in society brim with the great life force of Buddhas and bodhisattvas. Each of you, our noble members, is an entity of the Mystic Law. Please remember that, no matter where you are, that is the place for you to fulfill your mission from time without beginning.

Believe in the Gohonzon, the supreme object of
devotion in all of Jambudvipa [the entire world].
Be sure to strengthen your faith, and receive
the protection of Shakyamuni, Many Treasures,
and the Buddhas of the ten directions.

"The True Aspect of All Phenomena"
(WND-1, 386)

# THE UNSURPASSED GOOD FORTUNE
## AND BENEFIT OF FAITH

---

PRESIDENT TODA used to say quite matter-of-factly: "We deliberately chose to be born poor and sick so that we could spread the Mystic Law [through demonstrating the transformative power of faith to others.]"[11]

Our current circumstances are like a role we have taken on in this lifetime to fulfill our mission in accord with our eternal vow to lead others to happiness. Since we have embraced faith in the Gohonzon, the supreme object of devotion in the entire world, there is no adverse situation we cannot overcome. Let's activate the protective functions of the universe and win without fail.

Worthy persons deserve to be called so because they are not carried away by the eight winds: prosperity, decline, disgrace, honor, praise, censure, suffering, and pleasure.

*"The Eight Winds"*

**(WND-1, 794)**

# FORGING A SOLID AND UNSHAKABLE SELF

FAITH IN Nichiren Buddhism enables us to forge a solid and unshakable self. A life easily swayed by short-term gain or loss and the opinions of others is shallow and empty. Those who dedicate themselves unwaveringly to the great vow for kosen-rufu for the sake of people's happiness and the welfare of society are people of genuine substance.

Please purposefully walk the path of your mission unaffected by the eight winds to the very end. When you do so, not only will you be protected by the positive forces of the universe, but you will be able to perform a proud and victorious drama of human revolution and write a history of triumph that is free of all regret.

Because we have put our trust in the Lotus Sutra . . .
though we may suffer for a while, ultimately delight
awaits us. It is like the case of a crown prince,
the only son of the king. Consider this: How can
he possibly fail to ascend the throne?

*"Protecting the Atsuhara Believers"*

**(WND-2, 882)**

# UNWAVERING OPTIMISM

NICHIREN SENT this wholehearted encouragement to his young disciple Nanjo Tokimitsu who strove throughout the Atsuhara Persecution in the same spirit as he did.

The conviction that we will win no matter how trying the present times and definitely attain Buddhahood—this is the unshakable belief that transforms karma into mission. Courageous faith transforms hardship into joy. Here we find the unwavering optimism of Nichiren Buddhism.

Wherever we dwell and practice the single vehicle, that place will be the Capital of Eternally Tranquil Light.

*"Reply to Sairen-bo"*

**(WND-1, 313)**

# JOYFULLY STRIVING
# WHERE WE ARE

NICHIREN DAISHONIN wrote these words while being subjected to extreme hardship in exile. The Land of Eternally Tranquil Light is not some far-off utopia. It exists here and now where we are striving for kosen-rufu with the same spirit as our mentor.

No matter how trying the struggles we may be facing, if our resolve in faith remains unshaken in the depths of our life, then we can definitely triumph over everything. Always remember that the Capital of Eternally Tranquil Light resides in that resolve.

With the appearance of this teaching, all the teachings advocated by the scholars and teachers of Buddhism during the Former and Middle Days of the Law will be like stars after sunrise, or an awkward apprentice beside a skilled craftsman. It is stated that once this teaching is revealed in this era, the Buddha images as well as the priests of the temples built in the Former and Middle Days will all lose their power to benefit people, and only this great teaching will spread throughout the entire land of Jambudvipa [the entire world]. Since all of you have a bond with this teaching, you should feel reassured.

*"Letter to Misawa"*

(WND-1, 896)

# THE BUDDHISM OF THE SUN
# SHINES OVER ALL HUMANITY

NICHIREN BUDDHISM IS the Buddhism of the sun that will illuminate the entire world into the eternal future. It is a teaching of limitless hope that enables us to surmount the challenges of any time or age.

We were born with a profound mission and a deep karmic connection to this great Buddhism. Let's walk the path of victory with confidence and joy, together with our fellow members around the world, holding high the banner of the Mystic Law.

I entreat the people of this country: Do not look down upon my disciples! If you inquire into their past, you will find that they are great bodhisattvas who have given alms to Buddhas over a period of eight hundred thousand million kalpas, and who have carried out practices under Buddhas as numerous as the sands of the Hiranyavati and Ganges rivers. And if we speak of the future, they will be endowed with the benefit of the fiftieth person,[12] surpassing that of one who gave alms to innumerable living beings for a period of eighty years. They are like an infant emperor wrapped in swaddling clothes, or a great dragon who has just been born. Do not despise them! Do not look on them with contempt!

*"On the Four Stages of Faith and the Five Stages of Practice"*

(WND-1, 788–89)

# EVERYONE HAS A NOBLE MISSION

Nichiren Daishonin asserts here that those who chant Nam-myoho-renge-kyo are supremely worthy of respect and must not be looked down upon.

I read these words together with members in different regions across Japan, including in the pioneering campaigns in Kansai and Yamaguchi, to encourage them in our shared struggle. Brimming with this conviction, we achieved unprecedented success in widely spreading the Mystic Law.

I hope you will pass this sense of pride and honor on to our precious future division members and those who are new to the practice. With utmost respect for our fellow members, let's forge ahead harmoniously and with confidence.

What is called faith is nothing unusual. Faith means putting one's trust in the Lotus Sutra, Shakyamuni, Many Treasures, the Buddhas and bodhisattvas of the ten directions, and the heavenly gods and benevolent deities, and chanting Nam-myoho-renge-kyo as a woman cherishes her husband, as a man lays down his life for his wife, as parents refuse to abandon their children, or as a child refuses to leave its mother.

*"The Meaning of Faith"*

(WND-1, 1036)

# SHINE AS BRIGHT SUNS
# OF HAPPINESS

---

FAITH IS ONE of the most natural expressions of the human heart. We can simply chant to the Gohonzon with the same spirit of devotion as one cherishes one's family or as a parent seeks to protect one's child.

Mothers of young children are striving valiantly amid often challenging realities. It is our immediate environment, our daily life, that forms the stage on which we live out our drama of human revolution.

I hope that, today again, you will wisely and cheerfully shine as bright suns of happiness!

# CHAPTER 6

## Dance of Kosen-rufu

I will be the pillar of Japan. I will be the eyes of Japan.
I will be the great ship of Japan. This is my vow,
and I will never forsake it!

*"The Opening of the Eyes"*

**(WND-1, 280–81)**

## PILLAR OF PEACE, STABILITY, AND PROSPERITY

NICHIREN BUDDHISM, which is dedicated to establishing the correct teaching for the peace of the land, has immense importance. Today, the Soka Gakkai—an organization directly connected to the Daishonin—is the pillar, the eyes, and the great ship of Japan. It is unshakable. It is a positive force leading society in the direction of peace, stability, and prosperity amid turbulent times.

Neither the pure land nor hell exists outside oneself;
both lie only within one's own heart. Awakened to this,
one is called a Buddha; deluded about it, one is
called an ordinary person. The Lotus Sutra
reveals this truth, and one who embraces the
Lotus Sutra will realize that hell is itself the
Land of Tranquil Light.

*"Hell Is the Land of Tranquil Light"*

**(WND-1, 456)**

# A BUDDHA IS ONE WHO
# CONTINUES TO STRIVE

---

A BUDDHA IS not some kind of special, transcendent being. A Buddha is a person who continues to strive in the real world based on the Mystic Law, guided by the belief that one's own life and the lives of others are infinitely valuable and worthy of respect.

What distinguishes a Buddha from an unenlightened person is the unshakable conviction that one's inner potential is as vast as the universe itself. When we awaken to this truth, we will not be defeated by even the most challenging environment, and we will be able to make the place where we are right now shine as the Land of Tranquil Light.

As I have said before, be millions of times
more careful than ever.

*"The Hero of the World"*

**(WND-1, 839)**

# ALWAYS STAYING ALERT

CARELESSNESS IS our greatest enemy. We must safeguard against all accidents, particularly when there is an increased momentum in our activities. It is important to chant for no mishaps and to be alert to the smallest detail.

While deeply engraving in our hearts the Daishonin's words "be millions of times more careful," let's show actual proof that Buddhism means winning.

How far can our own wisdom take us? If we have even
enough wisdom to distinguish hot from cold,
we should seek out a good friend.

"Three Tripitaka Masters Pray for Rain"
**(WND-1, 598)**

# GOOD FRIENDS ON THE PATH OF HUMAN REVOLUTION

---

Our organization is a wonderful gathering of "good friends" in the realm of Buddhism. The Daishonin would certainly offer high praise for our discussion meetings where people of all ages and walks of life come together as equals to encourage and support one another.

When we advance in solid unity as good friends on the path of human revolution, the power of the Buddha will unfailingly manifest in our lives and we will be able to overcome any difficulty.

I do not know how to thank you for the sincerity you have shown in sending these articles. In the end, it must be an indication of the depth of the late Nanjo's faith in the Lotus Sutra. This is what is meant by the statement that a minister proclaims his ruler's sincerity, while a son proclaims his father's sincerity. The late Nanjo is probably delighted.

"The Story of Ohashi no Taro"

(WND-1, 675)

# FOSTERING SUCCESSORS IN FAITH IN THE FAMILY

---

NICHIREN SINCERELY praised the fostering of successors in the family, the solid transmission of faith from parent to child. The continuation of a deep commitment to kosen-rufu by the next generation will not only become a firm foundation for that whole family's enduring prosperity, but it will also serve as a bright source of hope for the community in which they live.

I hope that each Soka family will create its own wonderful history of kosen-rufu. Please remember that truly precious treasures of the heart—such as the courageous spirit to never be defeated by adversity and a warm spirit of care and concern for others—are imparted to children through the parents' example.

Being filial toward one's father and mother means that . . . one . . . is always mindful of providing a parent with all manner of good things, and if this happens to be impossible, in the course of a day one at least smiles twice or thrice in their direction.

*"The Four Virtues and the Four Debts of Gratitude"*

**(WND-2, 636)**

# BEING GOOD TO YOUR PARENTS

M Y YOUNG SUCCESSORS of the future division, cheerfully advance putting your studies and your health first.

Just seeing your bright and happy smiling faces can give your parents peace of mind and lift their spirits. There is nothing complicated about it; you can put into practice this supremely noble principle of being good sons and daughters with a simple, kind gesture. After all, the heart is what matters most.

I have believed it is most important to understand one's obligations to others, and made it my first duty to repay such debts of kindness. In this world, we owe four debts of gratitude. One who understands this is worthy to be called human, while one who does not is no more than an animal.

"Conversation between a Sage and an Unenlightened Man"

(WND-1, 122)

# REPAYING DEBTS OF GRATITUDE

Nichiren Buddhism teaches the correct human path of recognizing one's debts of gratitude and striving to repay them. President Toda, too, trained us so we would grow into people of first-rate character and outstanding members of society. Youth, please develop genuine ability! I hope you will always make your way through life with a sense of gratitude, and be sincere and respectful in your interactions with others.

If the Law that one embraces is supreme, then the person who embraces it must accordingly be foremost among all others. And if that is so, then to speak ill of that person is to speak ill of the Law.

*"Questions and Answers about Embracing the Lotus Sutra"*

**(WND-1, 61)**

# PEOPLE WHO SPREAD
# THE CORRECT TEACHING
# ARE SUPREMELY NOBLE

WE SHOULD PONDER the question "What is it that makes a person truly great?"

A person upholding a philosophy of the highest humanism is supremely noble. Therefore, as practitioners of Nichiren Buddhism working tirelessly for kosen-rufu, we have no need to feel intimidated by those in positions of power or authority. Moreover, we can bring forth limitless wisdom and strength to win over our real challenges and struggles.

Since childhood, I, Nichiren, have never prayed for the secular things of this life but have single-mindedly sought to become a Buddha. Of late, however, I have been ceaselessly praying for your sake to the Lotus Sutra, Shakyamuni Buddha, and the god of the sun, for I am convinced that you are a person who can inherit the soul of the Lotus Sutra.

*"The Hero of the World"*
**(WND-1, 839)**

# FOSTERING PRECIOUS SUCCESSORS

"ALL OF MY fellow practitioners who are striving for kosen-rufu are irreplaceable treasures who will inherit the essence of the Mystic Law. I must, therefore, support and protect them at all costs!"—this is the profoundly compassionate spirit of Nichiren Daishonin.

If we strive with this same spirit, then the SGI will eternally advance in triumph. Together, let's exert even greater efforts to encourage and foster our youth division and future division members— our precious successors who will "inherit the soul of the Lotus Sutra."

The seeds of one kind of plant are all the same; they are different from the seeds of other plants. If all of you nurture the same seeds of Myoho-renge-kyo in your hearts, then you all will be reborn together in the same land of Myoho-renge-kyo. When . . . you are reunited there face to face, how great your joy will be!

*"Reply to the Mother of Ueno"*
**(WND-1, 1074)**

# THE HAPPINESS OF OUR FAMILIES

---

FAMILY MEMBERS UNITED by the Mystic Law will definitely be reborn together again in a land where the Mystic Law is propagated. We can live out our lives forever with our families, our hearts never separated for even a moment.

The greatest thing that we can do for loved ones who have passed away is to confidently continue our work for kosen-rufu. While wholeheartedly chanting for the deceased, please develop a lofty life state together as a family, pervaded by the four noble virtues of eternity, happiness, true self, and purity.

Exert yourself in the two ways of practice and study.
Without practice and study, there can be no
Buddhism. You must not only persevere yourself;
you must also teach others. Both practice and
study arise from faith. Teach others to the
best of your ability, even if it is only
a single sentence or phrase.

*"The True Aspect of All Phenomena"*
**(WND-1, 386)**

# EXERT YOURSELF IN THE TWO WAYS OF PRACTICE AND STUDY

THE WRITINGS of Nichiren Daishonin are teachings of hope. When we study these writings and chant Nam-myoho-renge-kyo, our lives come to shine all the more brightly and overflow with courage, the wisdom of the Mystic Law, and the power of the Buddha.

The Daishonin encourages us to talk to others about Buddhism. Let's vibrantly reach out to others in dialogue. The more we talk to others about our practice, the more people we can help form a connection with Nichiren Buddhism, and the more benefit we can accumulate.

It is through exerting ourselves in the two ways of practice and study that we lay the foundation for victory for both our own lives and kosen-rufu.

The heart of the Lotus Sutra is the revelation that one may attain supreme enlightenment in one's present form without altering one's status as an ordinary person. This means that without casting aside one's karmic impediments one can still attain the Buddha way.

*"Reply to Hakiri Saburo"*

**(WND-1, 410)**

# JUST AS WE ARE

THE PURPOSE OF Nichiren Buddhism is to enable us to shine with supreme humanity; it is not for us to become someone or something special, other than who we are.

The Lotus Sutra teaches that we can attain Buddhahood in our present form, just as we are. When we earnestly practice Nichiren Buddhism just as we are, wisdom and power equal to that of the Buddha will well forth from within our lives.

From a mundane view, I am the poorest person in Japan, but in the light of Buddhism, I am the wealthiest person in all Jambudvipa [the entire world]. When I consider that this is all because the time is right, I am overwhelmed with joy and cannot restrain my tears. It is impossible to repay my debt of gratitude to Shakyamuni Buddha, the lord of teachings.

*"On Establishing the Four Bodhisattvas as the Object of Devotion"*

(WND-1, 977)

# CONFIDENTLY SPREADING NICHIREN BUDDHISM

A PERSON'S TRUE wealth is not determined by money or status but by their inner state of life.

We, who follow Nichiren's lead in upholding and practicing the Mystic Law, are also the wealthiest people in all the world. An indestructible Soka Gakkai has been built by ordinary people whose hearts are filled with the joy of propagating the Law.

Let's confidently continue to spread Nichiren Buddhism, with the happy pride of those who possess unsurpassed inner riches.

# CHAPTER 7

# Light of Fortune

When one carries out the single practice of
exercising faith in Myoho-renge-kyo, there are
no blessings that fail to come to one,
and no good karma that does not begin
to work on one's behalf.

"*Conversation between a Sage and
an Unenlightened Man*"
**(WND-1, 133)**

# MAKING POSITIVE CAUSES
## THROUGH OUR EFFORTS
### FOR KOSEN-RUFU

OUR EFFORTS to chant and spread Nam-myoho-renge-kyo produce myriad benefits and good causes, which multiply boundlessly when we all unite together in the shared prayer and aspiration for kosen-rufu. Not a single effort we put into our SGI activities is ever wasted.

That is why it's important that we bravely move forward based on faith and practice when we face obstacles or problems. Let's not forget that we can open the path to victory where we are right now through having the courage to take action.

At first one may seem to have faith in the Lotus Sutra,
but it is hard to maintain that faith to the last.
Water, for example, may be stirred by the wind,
or blossoms may lose their hue with the fading
of the morning dew. How, then, have you been
able to persist in your faith up until today?
It must be thanks entirely to the blessings you
have acquired in previous existences, and to the
care bestowed on you by Shakyamuni Buddha.
How heartening is that thought,
how heartening indeed!

*"The Buddha Resides in a Pure Heart"*
**(WND-2, 885)**

# IN PRAISE OF
# OUR PIONEER MEMBERS

---

As PIONEER MEMBERS who have striven wholeheartedly and made invaluable contributions to kosen-rufu, the wonderful benefits you have accumulated are undeniable and immeasurable. The Buddhas and bodhisattvas of the ten directions and three existences are surely praising and protecting you.

Even one seed, when planted, multiplies.

*"Cloth for a Robe and an Unlined Robe"*

**(WND-2, 602)**

## SEEDS OF THE MYSTIC LAW
## WILL BLOSSOM AS BENEFIT

WHEN WE TALK about Buddhism with our friends, we are planting and nurturing seeds of happiness in their lives as well as in our own. Let's make every effort to engage in conversation with one person after another.

These seeds planted through sincere and courageous efforts will produce beautiful flowers and fruit of benefit beyond anything we can imagine, bringing both our own lives and the lives of others to shine brilliantly.

To uphold the Lotus Sutra is the highest of all expressions of filial and supportive conduct.

*The Record of the Orally Transmitted Teachings*

**(OTT, 176)**

# THE HIGHEST MEANS OF SHOWING APPRECIATION TO OUR PARENTS

---

UPHOLDING THE Mystic Law enfolds our lives as well as those of our parents in limitless good fortune and benefit. It is the highest means of showing appreciation to our parents.

Even if your parents are not practicing Nichiren Buddhism, through the power of your prayer you will surely lead them to attain Buddhahood. In this way you will be able to fundamentally repay your debt of gratitude to them. And, for those of you who have lost a parent, chanting Nam-myoho-renge-kyo is the greatest way to offer prayers for their eternal happiness.

When our own life shines like the sun, we can illuminate not only our family, friends, and those in our environment, but also society as a whole.

SGI youth, please be good to your parents and always have a warm smile for them!

You also are a practitioner of the Lotus Sutra, and your faith is like the waxing moon or the rising tide. Be deeply convinced, then, that your illness cannot possibly persist, and that your life cannot fail to be extended! Take care of yourself, and do not burden your mind with grief.

*"The Bow and Arrow"*

(WND-1, 656)

# CHANTING WHOLEHEARTEDLY
## FOR GOOD HEALTH
## AND LONG LIFE

PRACTITIONERS OF the Lotus Sutra will never be defeated by illness—this firm conviction and strong resolve arise from faith in the Mystic Law. Even when battling a disease for a long time, please do not lose heart. In accord with the principle that Buddhas and bodhisattvas observe your efforts, Nichiren Daishonin is surely aware of all your struggles. There is no way that the positive forces of the universe will fail to protect you.

Please chant Nam-myoho-renge-kyo, bearing in mind the Daishonin's caution not to burden your mind with grief. Courageously overcome the devilish function of illness.

Today again, let's triumphantly pave the way for good health and long life with strength, wisdom, and optimism.

How can we possibly hold back our tears at the inexpressible joy of knowing that [at the moment of death] not just one or two, not just one hundred or two hundred, but as many as a thousand Buddhas will come to greet us with open arms!

*"The Heritage of the Ultimate Law of Life"*

**(WND-1, 216–17)**

## OUR JOURNEY ACROSS
## THE THREE EXISTENCES

---

THE COURSE OF our journey across the three existences of past, present, and future is peaceful yet vibrant. Because life and death are inseparable, the good fortune and benefit we have accumulated in this lifetime will last eternally. While we are alive, therefore, it is important that we continually strive to improve ourselves and take action for the welfare and happiness of others.

When your noble lives come to an end, you will be honored with the gratitude and respect of many, and protectively enfolded in the prayers of fellow members all around the globe.

The Buddha, being truly worthy of respect, never judges by the size of one's offerings. In the past, the boy Virtue Victorious offered a mud pie to the Buddha, and was reborn as King Ashoka and ruled over all of Jambudvipa [the entire world]. A poor woman cut off her hair and sold it to buy oil [for the Buddha], and not even the winds sweeping down from Mount Sumeru could extinguish the flame of the lamp fed by this oil.

*"Reply to Onichi-nyo"*

**(WND-1, 1089)**

# THE FLAME OF GOOD FORTUNE
## BURNS BRIGHTLY

T HE LAMP FUELED by the poor woman's sincere offering of oil could not be extinguished by even the most violent winds. In the same way, it is your dedicated efforts, fueled by the sincere desire for each person's happiness, that open the way to lasting victory.

No matter how fiercely the winds of adversity blow, they cannot put out the flame of good fortune that we have lit in our lives. Nor can the flame of the noble Mystic Law that we have lit in society ever be extinguished.

In the past, when the Buddha was still an ordinary mortal, in a turbulent age troubled by the five impurities he nourished the starving votaries of the Lotus Sutra and thereby was able to attain Buddhahood. And if the words of the Lotus Sutra are true, then because of the merit [you have gained by your gifts], there can be no doubt that your deceased father has already achieved Buddhahood.

*"The Beginning of Spring"*
**(WND-2, 982)**

# PRAYER FOR THE DECEASED

T HE BENEFIT we gain from dedicating ourselves to the cause of kosen-rufu in this impure
and troubled age shines with infinite brilliance—so
much so that it can even illuminate the lives of our
ancestors and descendants.

Therefore, as individuals striving for kosen-
rufu together with the SGI, our chanting of Nam-
myoho-renge-kyo itself is the supreme offering
we can make for the happiness of those who have
passed away. There is absolutely no doubt that
our deceased family and loved ones have already
attained Buddhahood.

Chanting Nam-myoho-renge-kyo is the true
way to confer benefit on the deceased in accord
with the essence of Nichiren Buddhism.

As I have often mentioned before, it is said that, where there is unseen virtue, there will be visible reward. Your fellow samurai all slandered you to your lord, and he also has wondered if it was true, but because you have for some years now honestly maintained a strong desire for your lord's welfare in his next life, you received a blessing like this. This is just the beginning; be confident that the great reward also is sure to come.

*"Unseen Virtue and Visible Reward"*

**(WND-1, 907)**

# BENEFIT SHINES IN SINCERITY

---

To earnestly continue chanting and taking action for the happiness of others, even if no one else sees our efforts—such unseen virtue will definitely bring clearly visible reward in the form of wonderful victory.

Always basing our actions on the Mystic Law—the fundamental law of cause and effect—we of the SGI have been able to win in every endeavor.

Nothing is ever wasted in our efforts for kosen-rufu. Those who are steadfast in their sincerity will triumph and prosper. Such is the realm of Nichiren Buddhism.

Should you depart from this life before I do,
you must report to Brahma, Shakra, the four heavenly
kings, and King Yama. Declare yourself to be a disciple
of the priest Nichiren, the foremost votary of the
Lotus Sutra in Japan. Then they cannot possibly
treat you discourteously.

*"Encouragement to a Sick Person"*

(WND-1, 82)

# A LIFE OF ETERNAL HONOR
# AND VICTORY

THE LIVES OF those who spread the Mystic Law and dedicate themselves to fulfilling the great vow for kosen-rufu are infinitely honorable and triumphant.

The good fortune we accumulate through such efforts will endure throughout the three existences of past, present, and future. We will definitely be protected in lifetime after lifetime. Our Buddhist practice as SGI members directly connected to the Daishonin is a source of brilliant and immeasurable benefit.

The sutra known as the Lotus Sutra is good medicine
for the various ills of body and mind. Thus it states:
"This sutra provides good medicine for the ills
of the people of Jambudvipa [the entire world].
If a person who has an illness is able to hear this
sutra, then his illness will be wiped out and
he will know neither old age nor death."[13]

*"On the Importance of the 'Expedient Means'
and 'Life Span' Chapters"*
**(WND-2, 747)**

# ROBUST AND CONFIDENT LIVES

WHAT ROBUST and confident lives we can lead when we possess the unsurpassed "good medicine" of the Mystic Law! We come to brim with greater vitality and grow more youthful in spirit with each passing year of our Buddhist practice. By manifesting the eternal Buddhahood innate within us, we can live undefeated by any obstacle or devilish function and savor health and longevity in our lives throughout the three existences of past, present, and future. Therefore, let's joyfully advance again today on the path of our mission!

# APPENDIX:
# LIST OF WORKS CITED

# NOTES

1. *The Lotus Sutra and Its Opening and Closing Sutras*, p. 178.
2. Referring to the passage in the "Encouraging Devotion," the 13th chapter of the Lotus Sutra: "At that time the bodhisattvas, respectfully complying with the Buddha's will and at the same time wishing to fulfill their own original vows, proceeded in the presence of the Buddha to roar the lion's roar and to make a vow" (LSOC, 231–32).
3. This statement is found in both the Nirvana Sutra and the Six Paramitas Sutra.
4. The Daishonin often uses Myoho-renge-kyo synonymously with Nam-myoho-renge-kyo in his writings.
5. *The Lotus Sutra and Its Opening and Closing Sutras*, p. 258.
6. This refers to the time when the Daishonin first proclaimed the teaching of Nam-myoho-renge-kyo.
7. Myoho-renge-kyo is written with five Chinese characters, while Nam-myoho-renge-kyo is written with seven (*nam,* or *namu,* being comprised of two characters). The Daishonin often uses Myoho-renge-kyo synonymously with Nam-myoho-renge-kyo in his writings.
8. The Japanese word for encouragement *hagemashi* is written with a Chinese character made up of the components "boundless" and "strength."

9. *The Lotus Sutra and Its Opening and Closing Sutras*, p. 233.
10. *The Lotus Sutra and Its Opening and Closing Sutras*, p. 273.
11. In the early days of the organization, the Soka Gakkai was often dismissed as a "gathering of the poor and sick."
12. Benefit of the fiftieth person: This refers to the immeasurable benefit obtained by even the fiftieth person in a chain of transmission who rejoices on hearing the Lotus Sutra.
13. *The Lotus Sutra and Its Opening and Closing Sutras*, p. 330.

# GLOSSARY

**Atsuhara Persecution**   A series of threats and acts of violence against followers of Nichiren Daishonin in Atsuhara Village, in Fuji District of Suruga Province, starting in around 1275 and continuing until around 1283. In 1279, the authorities executed three of Nichiren's followers for failing to renounce their faith.

**Bodhisattva Never Disparaging**   A bodhisattva described in "Bodhisattva Never Disparaging," the 20th chapter of the Lotus Sutra. He regarded all people with utmost respect because of their innate potential to become Buddhas.

**Bodhisattva Universal Worthy**   A bodhisattva who is regarded as symbolic of the virtues of truth and practice. In the "Universal Worthy," the 28th chapter of the Lotus Sutra, he vows to protect the Lotus Sutra and its votaries.

**Bodhisattvas of the Earth**   The innumerable bodhisattvas who appear in "Emerging from the Earth," the 15th chapter of the Lotus Sutra, and are entrusted by Shakyamuni with the task of propagating the Law after his passing. Nichiren regarded his followers who embrace and propagate the teaching of the Mystic Law as the Bodhisattvas of the Earth.

**Buddhahood**   The state of awakening a Buddha has attained. The ultimate goal of Buddhist practice. The word *enlightenment* is often used synonymously with Buddhahood.

**Buddha vehicle**   The teaching that leads all people to Buddhahood.

**Buddhas of the ten directions and three existences**   Ten directions refers to the entire universe, all physical space. The three existences indicate all of time. The expression "the Buddhas of the ten directions and three existences" in the sutras indicates all Buddhas throughout eternity and boundless space.

**changing poison into medicine**   The principle that earthly desires and suffering can be transformed into benefit and enlightenment by virtue of the power of the Law. This phrase is often cited to show that any problem or suffering can be transformed eventually into the greatest happiness and fulfillment in life.

**Devadatta**   A cousin of Shakyamuni who, after Shakyamuni's enlightenment, first followed him as a disciple but later became his enemy. In Buddhist scriptures, he is described as a man of utmost evil who tried to kill Shakyamuni Buddha and disrupt his Order.

**Eagle Peak**   A small mountain located northeast of Rajagriha, the capital of Magadha in ancient India. Eagle Peak is known as a place where Shakyamuni is said to have expounded the Lotus Sutra. Eagle Peak also symbolizes the Buddha land or the state of Buddhahood, as in the expression "the pure land of Eagle Peak."

**eight winds**   Eight conditions that prevent people from advancing along the right path to enlightenment. They are prosperity, decline, disgrace, honor, praise, censure, suffering, and pleasure.

**five impurities**   Also, five defilements. They refer to the impurity of the age, of desire, of living beings, of thought (or view), and of life span.

**Former, Middle Day, or Latter Day of the Law**   Three consecutive periods or stages into which the time following a Buddha's death is divided.

**four debts of gratitude**   The debts owed to one's parents, to all living beings, to one's sovereign, and to the three treasures of Buddhism.

**four heavenly kings**   In Buddhist mythology, the lords of the four quarters who are said to serve the god Shakra as his generals and protect the four quarters of the world.

**four kinds of believers**   Four categories of people who believe in Buddhism—monks, nuns, laymen, and laywomen.

**four noble virtues**   Four noble qualities of a Buddha's life—eternity, happiness, true self, and purity. These describe the true nature of a Buddha's life, which is pure and eternal, and which manifests the true self and enjoys absolute happiness.

**future division**   In the SGI, the future division consists of the members of the elementary and junior high and high school divisions.

**Gohonzon**   *Go* means "worthy of honor" and *honzon* means "object of fundamental respect." The object of devotion in Nichiren Buddhism and the embodiment of the Mystic Law permeating all phenomena.

**heavenly gods and benevolent deities** Also known as Buddhist gods, protective gods, protective functions. Gods who function to protect the people and their land and bring good fortune to both. Rather than primary objects of belief or devotion, Buddhism tends to view them as functioning to support and protect the Buddha, the Law, or Buddhist teachings, and practitioners. They can be viewed a manifestations of the Buddha nature in one's life and as the inherent functions of nature and society that protect those who uphold that Law.

**human revolution** A term employed by the Soka Gakkai's second president, Josei Toda, to indicate the self-reformation—the transformation of one's life and the attainment of Buddhahood—that is the goal of Buddhist practice.

**karma** Potentials in the inner, unconscious realm of life created through one's actions in the past or present that manifest themselves as various results in the present or future.

**King Yama** King Yama is king of the world of the dead who judges and determines the rewards and punishments of the deceased.

**kosen-rufu** A term from the Lotus Sutra that literally means "to declare and spread widely." Kosen-rufu refers to the process of securing lasting peace and happiness for all humankind by establishing the humanistic ideals of Nichiren Buddhism in society.

**Land of Tranquil Light** Also, Land of Eternally Tranquil Light. The Buddha land, or the land where the Buddha lives, which is free from impermanence and impurity.

**Lotus Sutra** A scripture of Mahayana Buddhism, it teaches that all people can reveal their innate Buddhahood and that this supreme potential is eternal. The sutra also encourages its practitioners to spread the teaching of universal Buddhahood and help all people awaken to this truth.

**Many Treasures Buddha** A Buddha depicted in the Lotus Sutra. Many Treasures appears, seated within his treasure tower, in order to lend credence to Shakyamuni's teachings in the sutra.

**Mother of Demon Children** A demoness said to have five hundred children. In "Dharani," the 26th chapter of the Lotus Sutra, she pledges before the Buddha to safeguard the votaries of the sutra.

**Mystic Law** (Jpn *myoho*) The ultimate Law, principle, or truth of life and the universe in Nichiren's teachings; the Law of Nam-myoho-renge-kyo. It has been translated also as Wonderful Law, Wonderful Dharma, Fine Dharma, etc.

**Nam-myoho-renge-kyo** The ultimate Law or truth of the universe, according to Nichiren's teaching. Nichiren teaches that this phrase encompasses all laws and teachings within itself and that the benefit of chanting Nam-myoho-renge-kyo includes the benefit of conducting all virtuous practices.

**protective functions** See *heavenly gods and benevolent deities*.

**pure land** A Buddha's land. The term is contrasted with *impure land*, meaning the saha world, or this world that is tainted with suffering and desire. A Buddha's land is said to be blissful and free from impurity and is therefore called a pure land.

**saha world**   This world, a world in which people must endure suffering. It is also defined as an impure land, a land defiled by earthly desires and illusion, in contrast with a pure land.

**Shakyamuni**   Also known as Gautama Buddha. The founder of Buddhism. "Shakyamuni" means "sage of the Shakyas," Shakya being the name of the tribe or clan to which his family belonged.

**ten demon daughters**   The ten female protective deities who appear in "Dharani," the 26th chapter of the Lotus Sutra, as the "daughters of rakshasa demons" or the "ten rakshasa daughters." They vow to the Buddha to guard and protect the sutra's votaries.

**Ten Worlds**:   Ten distinct realms or categories of beings referred to in Buddhist scriptures. The Lotus Sutra teaches that each of the Ten Worlds contains all ten within it, making it possible to interpret them as potential states of life inherent in each individual being.

**three powerful enemies**:   Three types of arrogant people who persecute those who propagate the Lotus Sutra in the evil age after Shakyamuni Buddha's death. The Great Teacher Miao-lo summarizes them as arrogant lay people, arrogant priests, and arrogant false sages.

**three existences of past, present, and future**:   Past existence, present existence, and future existence. Used to indicate all of time, from the eternal past, through the present, through the eternal future.

**Wonderful Law**   Also, the Mystic Law. The ultimate Law, principle, or truth of life and the universe in Nichiren's teachings; the Law of Nam-myoho-renge-kyo.

# INDEX